STUDY GUIDE

Contentment

Melissa Kruger

LIGONIER MINISTRIES

Renew your Mind.

LIGONIER.ORG | 800-435-4343

Copyright © 2018 Ligonier Ministries
421 Ligonier Court, Sanford, FL 32771
Email: info@ligonier.org
All rights reserved.
No reproduction of this work without permission.
Printed in China.

Contents

Introduction 3

Study Schedules 5

1. Biblical Contentment. 6

2. Defining Contentment. 13

3. The Source of Contentment. 20

4. The Enemy of Contentment. 27

5. What Causes Discontentment?. 34

6. Patterns of Discontentment. 41

7. An Example of Contentment. 48

8. Cultivating Contentment. 55

Introduction

It can be hard to be content. Our culture encourages us to covet and consume in ways that are contrary to biblical teaching. In *Contentment,* Melissa Kruger defines what biblical contentment is and what it means for the Christian life. She helps Christians recognize how the cultivation of contentment is fundamentally rooted in understanding and resting in the person and work of Jesus Christ. In Him, we find ultimate contentment.

This study guide is a companion to the video teaching series. Whether you are using the DVDs, streaming the videos on Ligonier.org, or going through the course in Ligonier Connect, this resource is designed to help you make the most of the learning experience. For each message in the series, there is a corresponding lesson in this guide. Here is what you will find in each lesson:

INTRODUCTION	The introduction is a brief paragraph that summarizes the content covered in the lecture and considered in the study guide lesson.
	How to use: Use the introduction to each lesson to get a sense of the big picture before watching the video. Refer to these statements as you work through the study guide to remind you of what have already covered and where you are headed.
LEARNING GOALS	The learning goals are the knowledge and skills the study guide lesson will endeavor to equip you with as you work through the lecture content.
	How to use: Familiarize yourself with the goals of each lesson before engaging its contents. Keeping the overall purpose in mind as you watch each video and reflect on or discuss the questions will help you get the most out of each lesson.
KEY IDEAS	The key ideas are the major points or takeaways from the lecture.
	How to use: Use these ideas to prepare yourself for each lesson and to review previous lessons. They describe specifically the knowledge each lecture is communicating.

REFLECTION & DISCUSSION QUESTIONS	The questions are the guided reflection and/or discussion component of the lesson that are intended to help you prepare for, process, and organize what you are learning. **How to use:** Reflect on individually or discuss in a group the questions in the order in which they appear in the lesson. The timestamps in the right margin indicate where the answers to questions during the video can be found.
PRAYER	The prayer section offers suggestions for how to close the lesson in prayer with respect to what was taught in the lecture. **How to use:** Consider using each lesson's prayer section as a guide to personal or group prayer. These sections follow the ACTS prayer model, which you can learn more about in R.C. Sproul's Crucial Questions booklet *Does Prayer Change Things?* This helpful guide is available as a free e-book at Ligonier.org.
REVIEW QUIZ	The review quiz is a set of six multiple-choice questions that appear at the end of each lesson. **How to use:** Use each quiz to check your comprehension and memory of the major points covered in each lecture. It will be most beneficial to your learning if you take a lesson's quiz either sometime between lessons or just before you begin the next lesson in the study guide.
ANSWER KEY	The answer key provides explanations for the reflection and discussion questions and answers to the multiple-choice questions in the review quiz. **How to use:** Use the answer key to check your own answers or when you do not know the answer. Note: Do not give in too quickly; struggling for a few moments to recall an answer reinforces it in your mind.

Study Schedules

The following table suggests four plans for working through the *Contentment* video teaching series and this companion study guide. Whether you are going through this series on your own or with a group, these schedules should help you plan your study path.

	Extended 10-Week Plan	Standard 8-Week Plan	Abbreviated 6-Week Plan	Intensive 4-Week Plan
Week	Lesson			
1	*	1	1	1 & 2
2	1	2	2	3 & 4
3	2	3	3 & 4	5 & 6
4	3	4	5 & 6	7 & 8
5	4	5	7	
6	5	6	8	
7	6	7		
8	7	8		
9	8			
10	*			

* For these weeks, rather than completing lessons, spend your time discussing and praying about your learning goals for the study (the first week) and the most valuable takeaways from the study (the last week).

1

Biblical Contentment

INTRODUCTION

Contentment is not a new longing. It has been desired and written about throughout history. Time and again, Scripture encourages believers to take heart through their circumstances and find contentment in the Lord. But what are the qualities of such a contentment and why is contentment important for believers today? In this lesson, Melissa Kruger explores what true contentment is and why it is important for us to study the topic of biblical contentment.

LEARNING GOALS

When you have finished this lesson, you should be able to:

- Describe three reasons why contentment is important
- Give a biblical definition of contentment
- Summarize three characteristics of contentment
- Recognize in Scripture where contentment is demonstrated and illustrated

KEY IDEAS

- Contentment cannot be found in anything—even in good things—apart from our eternal God.
- Our inward contentment should be outwardly apparent, so that we might be "spectacles of glory."
- True contentment is contingent not upon outward circumstances but upon the inward assurance of God's sovereignty.
- Jesus is the source of our contentment, just as the stream nourishes the tree in Psalm 1.

REFLECTION & DISCUSSION QUESTIONS

Before the Video

What Do You Think?

Take a moment to answer the following questions. They will prepare you for the lecture.

- Why are you undertaking this study? What do you hope to learn about contentment?

- How have you responded in the past to the hardships in your life?

Scripture Reading

But the fruit of the Spirit is love, joy, peace, patience, kindness, goodness, faithfulness, gentleness, self-control; against such things there is no law. And those who belong to Christ Jesus have crucified the flesh with its passions and desires. If we live by the Spirit, let us also keep in step with the Spirit. Let us not become conceited, provoking one another, envying on another.

—Galatians 5:22–26

- How might this passage motivate us to abide in the Word of God?

During the Video

Answer the following questions while you watch the video. They will guide you through the lecture.

Why Is Contentment Important?   *0:00–14:24*

- How does Mrs. Kruger's analogy of the woman standing before the ocean allude to how we can wrongly view contentment?

- Why does it matter that we be a people who exude hope?

- What does it mean that contentment is sourced inward and works outward?

Contentment Defined   *14:24–23:04*

- How does God's character inform our contentment?

- How is it that true contentment is independent of circumstances?

- How do trusting in the Lord and delighting in His Word relate to each other?

After the Video

Answer the following questions after you have finished the lecture. They will help you identify and summarize the major points.

- How does contentment influence how we pray?

> If you are in a group, have the members discuss what their prayer lives would look like if they asked that their hearts be changed before their circumstances.

- With the truth of God's grace in mind, why do you think we still struggle with viewing ourselves as "dry brittle branches"?

> If you are in a group, have the members consider the imagery of the tree in Psalm 1 and the fruit of the Spirit in Galatians 5 and ask what they think these metaphors say about us as people.

- What does Mrs. Kruger want us to learn from the story of her friend and her son's illness?

> If you are in a group, have each member discuss how they can help and serve the people they know who are going through hard circumstances.

PRAYER

Commit what you have learned from God's Word in this lesson to prayer.

- Praise God for His sovereignty over all things, His working all things according to His purposes.
- Confess how often you look to what is created to satisfy us in a way that only the Creator can.
- Thank God for not leaving you in your despair but giving you hope in Christ.

- Ask God to help you understand what contentment would look like in your life today.

REVIEW QUIZ

Use these multiple-choice questions to measure what you learned from this lesson.

1. Which of the following statements was *not* presented as a reason why contentment is an important topic to study?
   a. Our hope matters to the watching world.
   b. Christians need to be happy all the time.
   c. The church would be encouraged.
   d. Jesus cares about our joy.

2. In Psalm 1, why will the tree prosper and not wither?
   a. The shade protects it.
   b. A gardener tends to it.
   c. It is planted by the stream.
   d. It is in the area with the most sun.

3. Which of the following is *not* an accurate statement about contentment?
   a. It is an inward assurance of God's sovereignty.
   b. It is passed from one person to another.
   c. It is rooted in God's character.
   d. It is dependent on circumstances.

4. What must we also delight in to have true contentment?
   a. Ourselves
   b. God's Word
   c. Earthly blessings
   d. Loved ones

5. Contentment is a new desire that believers in the modern world are grasping for more than past generations did.
   a. True
   b. False

6. What does Mrs. Kruger describe this lesson on contentment as an intersection of?
   a. Real life intersecting with hard doctrine
   b. Real life intersecting with emotions
   c. Real life intersecting with real truth
   d. Real life intersecting with theory

Answer Key—Biblical Contentment

REFLECTION & DISCUSSION QUESTIONS

Before the Video

What Do You Think?

> *These are personal questions. The answers should be based on your own knowledge and experience.*

Scripture Reading

- How might this passage motivate us to abide in the Word of God?

> *This passage demonstrates that it is those who abide in God's Word that actually come to know God better, and find that true joy, peace, and patience come from Him. If we really want to possess the fruit of contentment, then we must seek the Lord where He has revealed Himself.*

During the Video

Why Is Contentment Important?

- How does Mrs. Kruger's analogy of the woman standing before the ocean allude to how we can wrongly view contentment?

> *Just as the woman wrongly thought that the ocean could quench her thirst, we can wrongly look to things to provide us joy and happiness other than the Lord. The ocean can be enjoyed and seen in a positive light in many different ways, but it is actually harmful to us if we look to it to provide things that it is not meant to. Looking for contentment in the wrong places will actually make us long for contentment more.*

- Why does it matter that we be a people who exude hope?

> *It matters that we be a people who exude hope, because the world watches how we live before it asks why we live the way that we do. To see a person living with joy in the midst of hard circumstances in a broken world is intriguing to the those who do not know Christ. Living in hope allows us to be able to give an answer for our hope.*

- What does it mean that contentment is sourced inward and works outward?

> *To trust that the Lord is sovereign is to be fully convinced inwardly that God is able to do all that He has promised (Rom. 4:21). The heart that trusts in God's rule and faithfulness is like the heart that is pumped with the life of Christ, which flows into all of our members. Contentment is an outward example of an inward work in our hearts.*

Contentment Defined

- How does God's character inform our contentment?

  Contentment is placing our trust and our hope in a God who is both good and sovereign. Discontentment breeds trust in false gods (money, relationships, etc.) and only intensifies our spiritual thirst. God's character speaks to who God is, so knowing that God is good and sovereign helps to root our contentment.

- How is it that true contentment is independent of circumstances?

  The thought that getting our circumstances right will solve all the problems in our lives is a lie that we often believe. We can tend to view our circumstances as the things we can control, but a contented heart recognizes our desperate condition and seeks to live in light of God's grace. This means that we pray for circumstances and care about circumstances, but we also understand that our contentment is rooted in the One who controls our circumstances no matter how our circumstances turn out.

- How do trusting in the Lord and delighting in His Word relate to each other?

  A person who trusts in the Lord is going to want to know the Lord more intimately. This means that someone who trusts in the Lord will meditate on His Word. Contented people will rightly be people who are regularly in the Word and meditating on it.

After the Video

- How does contentment influence how we pray?

  Having a heart that is content in our sovereign Lord allows us to examine ourselves before our circumstances. Instead of praying that our situation would change, we are first able to ask that the Lord would change our hearts and mold them more and more into the image of Christ. It is prayers like these that demonstrate our dependence on the Lord and acknowledge that He is working all circumstances for our ultimate good.

- With the truth of God's grace in mind, why do you think we still struggle with viewing ourselves as "dry brittle branches"?

  The answer to this question will differ slightly based on personal experience. One reason could be that we doubt God and think too lowly of His changing and sustaining power through the work of the Holy Spirit.

- What does Mrs. Kruger want us to learn from the story of her friend and her son's illness?

  Mrs. Kruger wants us to learn that, though her friend and her son are going through hard circumstances, God promises that He will be with her and strengthen her for everything she needs. Her friend realized that her joy comes from God, so she can pray fervently that God would change her hard circumstances while also shining as a spectacle of glory to the watching world.

REVIEW QUIZ

1. **B.**
   Christians are not expected to be happy all the time. Jesus was sorrowful and angry at times. As believers face difficult situations, real and numerous emotions are normal. Contentment goes beyond emotions and is not dependent on emotions.

2. **C.**
   The tree is planted by the stream and gets its nourishment from the constant source of water. While other trees wither during drought, this tree is rooted near its source of nourishment. Believers are to be rooted in Christ, who provides our nourishment so that we can prosper.

3. **D.**
   Hard circumstances come for every believer, however, contentment is not dependent on living an easy life. We should be content in spite of difficult circumstances.

4. **B.**
   Scripture is how God reveals Himself to and comforts believers. Without finding comfort and trust in the Lord from His Word, we cannot find true contentment.

5. **B.**
   The topic of contentment is addressed throughout Scripture and has been written about by Christian authors throughout history. In fact, humanity was created with a need for contentment. Every person who has ever existed longs for something to quench his need and provide contentment.

6. **C.**
   Contentment is not just a nice idea that is impossible to obtain. Real life gets messy and hard times come, but contentment is still obtainable. Our real, messy, difficult lives can still intersect with the truth of contentment.

2

Defining Contentment

INTRODUCTION

In order to gain contentment, believers must not only understand what it is but also what it is not. Through the help of Scripture, specifically the writings of the Apostle Paul, Christians are able to understand contentment and be encouraged on how to achieve it in their own lives. In this lesson, Melissa Kruger explains four characteristics of contentment, what contentment is not, and how to take heart through failure and hardship.

LEARNING GOALS

When you have finished this lesson, you should be able to:

- Describe four characteristics of contentment
- Explain four misconceptions about contentment
- Understand how the Apostle Paul's life can influence our contentment

KEY IDEAS

- Contentment is not just for Apostles and profound men of faith; it is for every Christian.
- Finding contentment in plenty is just as difficult as finding it in trials.
- Contentment is a learned skill, such that our circumstances are used to help us learn how to be content through whatever may come.
- Paul's life and the writings of the New Testament are a beacon of contentment and example to all believers for how to find true contentment.

REFLECTION & DISCUSSION QUESTIONS

Before the Video

What Do You Think?

Take a moment to answer the following questions. They will prepare you for the lecture.

- Do you think failure is important to the Christian life? How so?

- Who is someone you look to as a model of biblical contentment?

Scripture Reading

For we know that if the tent that is our earthly home is destroyed, we have a building from God, a house not made with hands, eternal in the heavens. For in this tent we groan, longing to put on our heavenly dwelling, if indeed by putting it on we may not be found naked. For while we are still in this tent, we groan, being burdened—not that we would be unclothed, but that we would be further clothed, so that what is mortal may be swallowed up by life. He who has prepared us for this very thing is God, who has given us the Spirit as a guarantee.

—2 Corinthians 5:1–5

- Why are contentment and longing for eternity not in opposition to one another?

During the Video

Answer the following questions while you watch the video. They will guide you through the lecture.

What Contentment Is   *0:00–15:43*

- How should knowing that the Spirit who raised Jesus from the dead now lives in us affect our view of contentment?

- How does learning about the life of Paul bring comfort to the modern Christian?

- In what ways can understanding our own weakness help us to be more content?

What Contentment Isn't   *15:43–23:18*

- How can sharing our burdens with other believers help both us and them to find contentment?

- What are helpful things that we can say to members of our community going through hardships and difficult circumstances?

- How does knowing that contentment is not the absence of fear help you to better handle your own fears and anxieties?

After the Video

Answer the following questions after you have finished the lecture. They will help you identify and summarize the major points.

- Thomas Watson says that a contented Christian is one who is "captivated under the authority of the Word." Why is it important for the Christian to see themselves as under authority to the Word when pursuing contentment?

If you are in a group, have the members discuss what a cheerful life would look like for each of them. Discuss what would be at the center of that cheerfulness.

- Do you find it hard to bear the burdens of a brother or sister in Christ when they are suffering? What do you think is at the root of such a struggle to be empathetic and compassionate?

If you are in a group, have the members name a time when it was difficult to show compassion to someone going through hardship and what they learned about themselves through that experience.

- Why do we often believe that plenty and comfort will bring us contentment? How are we misunderstanding what it is to be content?

If you are in a group, have each member think of examples where having plenty actually made them less content instead of more content.

PRAYER

Commit what you have learned from God's Word in this lesson to prayer.

- Praise God for giving you a community in which you can share your burdens and hardships.
- Confess how often you desire things rather than the God who created us.
- Thank God for giving you His Spirit to work in you and to show you your weaknesses.
- Ask God to help you learn that your weakness is being used by God even now to conform you to His image.

REVIEW QUIZ

Use these multiple-choice questions to measure what you learned from this lesson.

1. Which of the following is *not* an accurate statement about contentment?
    a. Contentment isn't a carefree existence.
    b. Contentment isn't the absence of relational struggles.
    c. Contentment isn't a life without longing.
    d. Contentment isn't for every Christian.

2. Which of the following biblical figures is mentioned as a beacon of contentment?
    a. Luke
    b. David
    c. Moses
    d. Paul

3. What is Paul referring to when he wrote, "I can do all things through him who strengthens me" (Phil. 4:13)?
    a. His trials
    b. His abilities
    c. His contentment
    d. His longings and desires

4. What reason did Mrs. Kruger give as to why having plenty does not bring contentment?
    a. Having plenty does not test believers.
    b. We will just want more and more blessings.
    c. God did not design us to be content in plenty.
    d. Having plenty has unforeseen trials of its own.

5. God does not require us to be content; contentment is an added bonus.
    a. True
    b. False

6. Why, according to this lesson, will Christians always be longing?
    a. We are sinful creatures.
    b. We can never be content.
    c. We were created for a different place.
    d. God did not give us the ability to be content.

Answer Key—Defining Contentment

REFLECTION & DISCUSSION QUESTIONS

Before the Video

What Do You Think?

These are personal questions. The answers should be based on your own knowledge and experience.

Scripture Reading

- Why are contentment and longing for eternity not in opposition to one another?

    As Christians, we are designed to long for eternity. This does not mean, however, that God does not want us to be content in this world. To be content in this world is to have our greatest joy still future—dwelling in the presence of the Lord forever. To be content in this world is to have our priorities in proper order.

During the Video

What Contentment Is

- How should knowing that the Spirit who raised Jesus from the dead now lives in us affect our view of contentment?

    All Christians possess the same Spirit, and the Spirit's presence and work reminds us that the Spirit who is within us is greater than our flesh. No matter how we might feel about ourselves, we are encouraged to remember that our internal war with sin can and ultimately will be won. It is the hope of the power of the Spirit that informs our contentment.

- How does learning about the life of Paul bring comfort to the modern Christian?

    Paul's description of his life is one that includes a multitude of hard circumstances. Paul's life was difficult, and he knew and experienced things that many of us will likely never experience in this life, and yet Paul always pointed people back to Christ through a retelling of his circumstances. Paul was not concerned with showing how great he was but with showing how Christ's strength is made perfect in weakness.

- In what ways can understanding our own weakness help us to be more content?

    As it was with Paul, so it is with us: our weakness serves to show the strength and glory of Christ. Our weakness shows that Christ is still working in us by His Spirit and making us more and more like Himself. Therefore, we can be content with where we currently are, though never complacent with where we are, knowing that Christ is creating in us hearts that are more patient, kind, compassionate, humble, and meek.

What Contentment Isn't

- How can sharing our burdens with other believers help both us and them to find contentment?

  Understanding that life is burdensome and hard can be debilitating if it is not coupled with an understanding of community. If we do not have others with whom to share our burdens, then we will be crushed under their weight. To acknowledge hardships and to seek to live faithfully through them is not antithetical to contentment but is a solid foundation for it.

- What are helpful things that we can say to members of our community going through hardships and difficult circumstances?

  This answer will vary based on your experience, but some helpful things to say could include simply acknowledging that life is hard. It is not our duty to sugarcoat the reality of what someone is going through, but instead it is our duty to listen to, pray with, weep with, and be with a person who is experiencing hardships. This is hard for many of us, because we think we can be more helpful than that, but we must remember that God is the true Comforter, the true Healer, and the true Helper. Our calling is to be faithful and to trust and pray for God to bring ultimate comfort.

- How does knowing that contentment is not the absence of fear help you to better handle your own fears and anxieties?

  This answer will vary depending on your experience, but it might be helpful to consider that fear is not something to be avoided but to be faced head on. Fear can only be faced rightly when it is coupled with contentment that seeks the Lord in all things. The Lord is the One who gives us strength not to fear, though we walk through the valley of the shadow of death. No one is without fear in this life, but through the strength that Christ supplies, we can walk ahead boldly.

After the Video

- Thomas Watson says that a contented Christian is one who is "captivated under the authority of the Word." Why is it important for the Christian to see themselves as under authority to the Word when pursuing contentment?

  Since true contentment is found only in the Lord, then it logically follows that we can only learn contentment by sitting at the feet of our Lord and listening to Him. It is only in God's revealed Word that we can know what contentment is and why we should value it and pursue it. Therefore, we are to be a people under the authority of the Word so that we can learn contentment from the One who is the source of all contentment.

- Do you find it hard to bear the burdens of a brother or sister in Christ when they are suffering? What do you think is at the root of such a struggle to be empathetic and compassionate?

The answer to these questions should help you to consider how weak and selfish we can be and how that can cause us to distort our understanding of contentment.

- Why do we often believe that plenty and comfort will bring us contentment? How are we misunderstanding what it is to be content?

Our flesh desires satisfaction from things, people, and experiences. Our sinful hearts deceive us in this way by leading us to think that a lack of possessions is the issue. It is only when the Spirit searches our hearts that we see that our true lack is in holiness and righteousness. It is the killing of sin and drawing nearer to Christ that actually breeds contentment.

REVIEW QUIZ

1. **D.**
   Contentment is not reserved for Apostles and giants of the faith. Contentment is for every Christian. Mrs. Kruger states that it is a misconception to think of contentment as a carefree existence, a life without longing, or a life free of relational struggles.

2. **D.**
   Paul's life is a beacon to the modern Christian as an example of true contentment in the face of great trials and adversity.

3. **C.**
   In Philippians 4:13, Paul is referring not to his own strength but to his contentment. Once Paul had found contentment in Christ, he knew that he could weather any hardship that came his way because he had strength in Christ.

4. **D.**
   People often dream of earthly blessings and can easily believe that having money or finding a spouse will solve all their issues and bring contentment. However, these blessings come with trials of their own.

5. **B.**
   As Christians, we are commanded to be content, to be joyful, and to give thanks to the Lord. When we are not content, we are not obeying the Lord.

6. **C.**
   Believers should long for eternity. We were made to spend eternity with Christ, and so we, while on earth, will always be longing. When we are with God in eternity, we will no longer feel such longing.

The Source of Contentment

INTRODUCTION

God's characteristics are the source of our contentment. The attributes and characteristics of God allow us to rest and trust in Him completely. He is worthy of our hope and trust because of who He is. Our God is omniscient, omnipresent, omnipotent, self-sufficient, good, and just. In this lesson, Melissa Kruger discusses how the attributes and characteristics of God are the reason for and foundation of Christian contentment.

LEARNING GOALS

When you have finished this lesson, you should be able to:

- Name six characteristics of God related to contentment
- Define the terms *omniscient*, *omnipresent*, and *omnipotent*
- Explain why the source of our contentment is God Himself

KEY IDEAS

- God's characteristics enable and directly source our contentment.
- We are creatures and God is our Creator; He is worthy of all trust and praise.
- God's power strengthens believers in their weakness; He is more powerful than we are weak.

REFLECTION & DISCUSSION QUESTIONS

Before the Video

What Do You Think?

Take a moment to answer the following questions. They will prepare you for the lecture.

- How has it affected your thinking about contentment to learn about what contentment is not?

- What are some characteristics of God that help you to trust in the Lord and find contentment?

Scripture Reading

O Lord, you have searched me and known me! You know when I sit down and when I rise up; you discern my thoughts from afar. You search out my path and my lying down and are acquainted with all my ways. Even before a word is on my tongue, behold, O Lord, you know it altogether.

—Psalm 139:1–4

- What does this passage say to us about God's knowledge? Why is it important?

During the Video

Answer the following questions while you watch the video. They will guide you through the lecture.

Our All-Knowing, Ever-Present Creator   0:00–10:22

- What is a wrong way to understand God's omnipresence?

- Does God's relation to us as our Creator mean that He owes us a better life? Why or why not?

Powerful, Good, and Just   10:22–23:31

- "When we are weak, He is strong." How is this statement good news for the Christian?

- How does a life of thanksgiving allow the Christian to experience life in ways that are impossible to experience otherwise?

After the Video

Answer the following questions after you have finished the lecture. They will help you identify and summarize the major points.

- How should God's omniscience relate to our trust in Him?

  If you are in a group, discuss our tendency to question God's wisdom for our lives. What do we believe about ourselves when we think this way? In what areas of your life do you think too little of God—of His wisdom and His power?

- Why, more than His other characteristics, do God's promises rest in His goodness and sovereignty?

  If you are in a group, discuss areas in your life where you thought you could construct a better situation for yourself than you were presently experiencing. What did you learn at the end of that experience?

- What is the mystery of God's sovereignty? Why does it matter for our lives today?

  If you are in a group, have the members discuss where their lives would look different if they regarded God's sovereignty properly. What aspects of life would they appreciate more?

PRAYER

Commit what you have learned from God's Word in this lesson to prayer.

- Praise God for knowing you in every way far greater than you could ever know yourself.
- Confess ways in which you disregard God's goodness.
- Thank God for working all things together for the good of His people.
- Ask God to help you appreciate the life you have so that you live in thankfulness to Him.

REVIEW QUIZ

Use these multiple-choice questions to measure what you learned from this lesson.

1. Which of the following terms did Mrs. Kruger combine with the concept of self-sufficiency?
   a. Sacrifice
   b. Creature
   c. Creator
   d. Ruler

2. What does Mrs. Kruger say often leads to our discontentment?
   a. Our family
   b. God's characteristics
   c. The actions of others
   d. Our pride

3. What two characteristics do all the promises of God rest on?
   a. His grace and goodness
   b. His sovereignty and power
   c. His goodness and sovereignty
   d. His power and grace

4. Which of the following was *not* an attribute of God highlighted in this session?
   a. Oneness
   b. Omniscience
   c. Omnipotence
   d. Omnipresence

5. The death of Christ on the cross allowed God to be the just and the justifier.
   a. True
   b. False

6. What is the worst fate imaginable?
   a. Death
   b. Persecution
   c. An eternity without Christ
   d. Having those close to you perish

Answer Key—The Source of Contentment

Before the Video

What Do You Think?

These are personal questions. The answers should be based on your own knowledge and experience.

Scripture Reading

- What does this passage reveal to us about God's knowledge? Why is it important?

This passage reveals that God's knowledge is inexhaustible. He knows everything about His creation, from surface-level information such as our names to the intimate details of our lives. This is important, because it should rightly inform our understanding and reverence for God. He does not abuse His infinite knowledge but perfectly cares for His creatures in accordance with how He has made them.

During the Video

Our All-Knowing, Ever-Present Creator

- What is a wrong way to understand God's omnipresence?

It would be wrong to view God's omnipresence with fear and anxiety. God does not abuse His presence in our lives, seeking to manipulate and strike us down at the first sign of a mistake. God's omnipresence should instead be seen as a comfort to His people, because like a loving Father, He promises to be with us always. We should feel freedom and a proper boldness in coming to our heavenly Father.

- Does God's relation to us as our Creator mean that He owes us a better life? Why or why not?

Because God is our Creator, we are not to act as if we can dictate what God owes us based on our terms. Instead, we see that Jesus promises His followers troubles in this world, but we are encouraged to take heart, for He will be with us. God's position as Creator gives Him authority over our lives, not the other way around.

Powerful, Good, and Just

- "When we are weak, He is strong." How is this statement good news for the Christian?

Scripture teaches us that because we are creatures, we are dependent upon our Creator for everything. This applies to our strength as well. It is the one who recognizes his weakness and turns to God in humility that will receive the strength that God supplies. He is able to make us content, because His power is greater than our weakness.

- How does a life of thanksgiving allow the Christian to experience life in ways that are impossible to experience otherwise?

  Christians know that the debt for their sins has been paid and that God's justice has been met on their behalf. Christians are then set free to live a life free from guilt and the attempt to earn the righteousness they could never attain in and of themselves. Apart from the grace of God in Christ, it is impossible to look at God through any other lens than that of guilt and shame in the futile attempt to earn righteousness. A life of thanksgiving is a gift only a Christian can truly enjoy.

After the Video

- How should God's omniscience relate to our trust in Him?

  Because God is omniscient, we can know for certain that God does not make mistakes in how He governs our lives. He can see the beginning from the end and cares for us intimately, so our lives should always be oriented toward Him in faith.

- Why, more than His other characteristics, do God's promises rest in His goodness and sovereignty?

  We must know that God is good to be able to trust His character, but we must know that God is also sovereign to trust that He is able to carry out His good and perfect purposes. Otherwise, God may be good, but His promises are outside of His control. If He is not good but sovereign, then God could be rightly viewed as a tyrant. But God is both good and sovereign, so we can know that God is working all things together for good.

- What is the mystery of God's sovereignty? Why does it matter for our lives today?

  The mystery of God's sovereignty is that God reigns over all events and yet man is fully responsible for his actions. This matters for us, because it reminds us that only God is able to comprehend and reconcile these two seemingly irreconcilable truths. It helps us not to view God's actions only through the eyes of the present but to trust that He will work all things together for an ultimate and eternal good.

REVIEW QUIZ

1. **C.**
   God formed us in our mother's womb and knew everything about our lives even then. We were created by God and for God. He is self-sufficient and does not owe His creation anything.

2. **D.**
   We sometimes think that we could have created a better world than God did, or that we know better than Him in certain ways. This is a demonstration of our sinful pride and a sure road to discontentment.

3. **C.**

   God is all-powerful and rules over all things. This should not scare us, however, because we know that God is a good God who rules with righteousness. His goodness and sovereignty meet and work perfectly together as the sure foundation of His promises.

4. **A.**

   Mrs. Kruger highlighted six different characteristics of God in this session. God is omniscient, omnipresent, omnipotent, self-sufficient Creator, good, and just.

5. **A.**

   The cross was a display of God's love and justice. God does not excuse our sin, so He is just. In forgiving those who trust in Christ and His atoning work, He is also able to be our justifier. This is why the justice of God is a great source of our contentment, for in Christ, we truly are forgiven.

6. **C.**

   Death is not the worst fate imaginable. The worst fate imaginable is an eternity without Christ. No matter what happens to us each day, we have the knowledge that even death is not the worst fate. We get to live forever in eternity with Christ. We should then live each day in His light and in accordance with that knowledge.

4

The Enemy of Contentment

INTRODUCTION

Not only is it important to understand what contentment is and what it looks like, but it is also important to understand contentment's enemy. In this lesson, Melissa Kruger explores the sin of covetousness, how it threatens our contentment, and how we can recognize it in our own hearts. Covetousness is not a minor sin. It is one of the Ten Commandments and a great enemy of our contentment.

LEARNING GOALS

When you have finished this lesson, you should be able to:

- Define covetousness
- Describe three characteristics of covetousness
- List four ways to recognize the sin of covetousness in your own life
- Explain why covetousness is the enemy of contentment

KEY IDEAS

- One enemy of our contentment is covetousness, though we often do not view coveting with the same severity as other sins.
- There are both right desires and sinful desires of the heart; it is important to discern between them.
- Envy, lust, and greed are all different forms of covetousness; coveting is not limited to money and possessions.
- Covetousness is a dangerous, begetting sin marked by comparison and entitlement that is never solved by attainment.

REFLECTION & DISCUSSION QUESTIONS

Before the Video

What Do You Think?

Take a moment to answer the following questions. They will prepare you for the lecture.

- Do you struggle with covetous desires? How has this stirred discontentment in your life?

- Do you ever minimize the sin of covetousness? When have you done this in the past?

Scripture Reading

*Now the serpent was more crafty than any other beast of the field that the L*ORD *God had made. He said to the women, "Did God actually say, 'You shall not eat of any tree in the garden'?" And the woman said to the serpent, "We may eat of the fruit of the trees in the garden, but God said, 'You shall not eat of the fruit of the tree that is in the midst of the garden, neither shall you touch it, lest you die.'" But the serpent said to the woman, "You will not surely die. For God knows that when you eat of it your eyes will be opened, and you will be like God, knowing good and evil." So when the woman saw that the tree was good for food, and that it was a delight to the eyes, and that the tree was to be desired to make one wise, she took of its fruit and ate, and she also gave some to her husband who was with her, and he ate.*

—Genesis 3:1–6

- How did the sin of covetousness play a role in the fall of humanity?

During the Video

Answer the following questions while you watch the video. They will guide you through the lecture.

Coveting Defined   *0:00–7:34*

- How does rightly confessing our sin help us understand the gospel better?

- What does it mean that coveting is an "inordinate" desire? Can desires be inordinate?

The Effects of Coveting   *7:34–23:16*

- How can limiting the definition of coveting affect our understanding of contentment?

- Does Mrs. Kruger's point of living within the present season of life mean that looking toward and planning for the future is incompatible with contentment?

After the Video

Answer the following questions after you have finished the lecture. They will help you identify and summarize the major points.

- What does Mrs. Kruger mean when she says that "coveting is a sin pattern, not a circumstance"?

If you are in a group, discuss what you can be doing now to be putting to death the sin of blaming God instead of ourselves for the sins we commit.

- How has our expanded understanding of who our neighbor is affected our understanding of coveting and discontentment?

If you are in a group, discuss how social media in particular has had an effect on how you view your friends and neighbors.

- Why do we often think it is acceptable to complain and grumble in a season of waiting?

If you are in a group, have the members discuss areas in their lives where they are currently in a season of waiting. What have you felt the most temptation to complain about?

PRAYER

Commit what you have learned from God's Word in this lesson to prayer.

- Praise God for His forgiveness of your covetous desires and His new mercies each day.
- Confess the sinful desires of your heart and how coveting has led you to stray from contentment in your life.
- Thank God for the many blessings He has given to you, though you do not deserve them.

• Ask God to help you rejoice with others in their happiness instead of only desiring happiness for yourself.

REVIEW QUIZ

Use these multiple-choice questions to measure what you learned from this lesson.

1. What word is *not* used in the definition stated for coveting?
   a. Positive
   b. Desire
   c. Culpable
   d. Inordinate

2. Which of the following is *not* one of the three sins included under the umbrella of covetousness?
   a. Lust
   b. Greed
   c. Gluttony
   d. Envy

3. Why does Thomas Watson call coveting "a mother sin"?
   a. It is the greatest sin.
   b. It was the original sin.
   c. It is the sin we should care about the most.
   d. It gives birth to all other sin.

4. Which of the following is *not* a way to tell if a desire is sinful or sour?
   a. Our means of obtaining a good thing are wrong.
   b. Our attitude while waiting is wrong.
   c. We don't get our desire right away.
   d. The object of our desire is wrong.

5. When someone else has more success or blessings than you do, it means that God loves him more than He loves you.
   a. True
   b. False

6. What word does Mrs. Kruger use to describe the sin of covetousness from *The Rare Jewel of Christian Contentment*?
   a. Hard-heartedness
   b. Stubbornness
   c. Blasphemy
   d. Rebellion

Answer Key—The Enemy of Contentment

REFLECTION & DISCUSSION QUESTIONS

Before the Video

What Do You Think?

These are personal questions. The answers should be based on your own knowledge and experience.

Scripture Reading

- How did the sin of covetousness play a role in the fall of humanity?

  Eve looked at the tree of the knowledge of good and evil and desired to eat of it even though she was commanded not to. Coveting is a sin of the will, and we see this played out in Eve's believing the serpent's lie and believing that something was being kept back from her. Eve's covetous desire ultimately led her to act in disobedience, which not only did not bring her the thing she desired but also caused her to forfeit what she possessed before.

During the Video

Coveting Defined

- How does rightly confessing our sin help us understand the gospel better?

  The good news of the gospel is only good news because there is bad news. The bad news is that we are totally depraved sinners outside of the grace of Christ. The good news is that God has stretched out His mercies to a condemned and dead people and rescued them in Christ. If we do not look at our sin and confess it to be sin, then we do not really believe Christ is our Savior.

- What does it mean that coveting is an "inordinate" desire? Can desires be inordinate?

  It is thought by many in our day that our desires cannot be controlled and so no moral responsibilities should be attached to them. As Christians, however, we know this is not the case, for sin has just as much to do with our hearts as it does with our actions. Coveting, then, affects our hearts and turns the desires of our hearts into idols. We eventually come to desire the object more than the Giver. This is something that the Christian must always be warring against.

The Effects of Coveting

- How can limiting the definition of coveting affect our understanding of contentment?

Coveting involves so much more than just money or possessions, but for many of us, it may be difficult to believe that. We can covet another person's spouse, another person's family, another person's status. It doesn't even matter if we have an abundance of the things we desire; we can still covet and wrongly desire the one thing we don't have. Our understanding of contentment is then flawed, because we don't do full justice to the range of influence that coveting can have and where it can show up in our lives.

- Does Mrs. Kruger's point of living within the present season of life mean that looking toward and planning for the future is incompatible with contentment?

Longing for the next season in life is a very present danger for each of us. It is easy not to live with joy in the present because we are so anxious about attaining joy in the future. We must hold the proper tension, however, and recognize that contentment is enjoying God's mercies today while also seeking to live faithfully so that we can enjoy more daily mercies in the future. The two are not opposed but flow out of one another.

After the Video

- What does Mrs. Kruger mean when she says that "coveting is a sin pattern, not a circumstance"?

The heart of this issue gets back to what we believe about God's sovereignty and our sin. We can sometimes think that it is our circumstances that are holding us back from living rightly, when we are actually the problem. God could give us everything we ever wanted, yet if our hearts are not changed, our circumstances will always be hard. Sin that is not put to death never really goes away; it just takes on a new form. We must be committed, then, to addressing our sin and putting it to death.

- How has our expanded understanding of who our neighbor is affected our understanding of coveting and discontentment?

We live in a global society where we know more about what is going on in the world than ever before. This reality naturally widens the definition of who our neighbor is. Since we are prone to covet the things of those whom we see, it can often be the case that someone living in a completely different country has more of our attention than someone living across the street from us. This is something we must be aware of as we interact on social media and other platforms and see the different lives of people from all over the globe.

- Why do we often think it is acceptable to complain and grumble in a season of waiting?

This is one of the most telling tests of the state of our hearts. If we act as if we have a right to grumble over all of the things we do not have, it shows that our desires have become tainted. We don't desire to see what God is teaching us through this season of waiting but instead complain until we get what we want. This is not a sign of maturity and contentment but of immaturity and discontentment. Our desire should be to grow in dependence upon the Lord instead of dependence upon things.

REVIEW QUIZ

1. **A.**

   Coveting is never a positive desire. The Bible uses other words for good desires, but coveting is not one of them. Coveting is "an inordinate or culpable desire to possess often that which belongs to another."

2. **C.**

   Mrs. Kruger includes the sins of envy, lust, and greed under the broader term of coveting. Envy is coveting that looks at those around you and wants what they have. Lust is coveting of a sexual nature. Greed is coveting that always wants more. Greed mainly relates to money and possessions and never having enough.

3. **D.**

   Thomas Watson called coveting "a mother sin" because it gives birth to all other sins. Covetous desires don't stay inside our hearts. Sinful desires manifest themselves in our lives. The desires of our hearts lead to other sins.

4. **C.**

   There are four ways given in this lesson to identify if a desire is sinful or has turned sour. Those ways are that the object of our desire is wrong, the means we go about obtaining a good thing is wrong, the motivation for our desire is wrong, and our attitude while waiting is wrong. We are never promised that our desires will be granted right away, especially if they are sinful desires.

5. **B.**

   We should never look at another person's life, compare it to our own, and think that God loves him more than He loves us. Instead, we should trust in the Lord that He will provide for us. We ought to look at our neighbors and love them instead of questioning if God loves us.

6. **D.**

   Covetousness is rebellion against God. This rebellion shows that we do not trust in Him. In The Rare Jewel of Christian Contentment, *Jeremiah Burroughs says, "When you feel your heart discontented and murmuring against the dispensations of God towards you, you should check it thus: Oh you wretched heart! What, will you be a rebel against God? Will you rise in rebellion against the infinite God? Yet you have done so. Charge your heart with this sin of rebellion."*

5

What Causes Discontentment?

INTRODUCTION

What goes on in our hearts that causes us to be discontent? Why do we, as believers, struggle with discontentment? When we bring to light the sinful thoughts and desires of our hearts, it is easier to answer these questions, repent to the Lord, pray, and strive for change. In this lesson, we will study three sins that source our discontentment and how to overcome them.

LEARNING GOALS

When you have finished this lesson, you should be able to:

- Name the three sins at the heart of discontentment
- Understand how to biblically view this world and the world to come

KEY IDEAS

- When we covet, we miss what has been given to us, and we cannot enjoy God's blessings if we only focus on what we do not have.
- The source of discontentment is unbelief.
- When we covet, we are not believing that God is sovereign over all things.
- What Christ intends for our lives is better than whatever we can ask or think for our own lives.
- When we are discontent, we are saying that the cross of Christ is insufficient.

REFLECTION & DISCUSSION QUESTIONS

Before the Video

What Do You Think?

Take a moment to answer the following questions. They will prepare you for the lecture.

- Have you ever questioned something God was doing in your life? Do you look back on trials differently once they have passed?

- How could Christ's death on the cross affect the way you strive for contentment?

Scripture Reading

Trust in the LORD with all your heart, and do not lean on your own understanding. In all your ways acknowledge him and he will make straight your paths. Do not be wise in your own eyes; fear the LORD, and turn away from evil. It will be healing to your flesh and refreshment to your bones.

—Proverbs 3:5–8

- How does our estimation of our own wisdom affect our contentment?

During the Video

Answer the following questions while you watch the video. They will guide you through the lecture.

Discontentment   *0:00–13:10*

- How is discontentment a reflection of unbelief?

- How should the understanding that this world is not our home inform how we live in the present?

Purpose in Christ   *13:10–21:36*

- How is it good news that Christ's purpose for us is not to have our best life now?

- How can misunderstanding our purpose in the body of Christ produce discontentment?

After the Video

Answer the following questions after you have finished the lecture. They will help you identify and summarize the major points.

- What does discontentment say about our view of the cross?

  If you are in a group, discuss how seriously you take the issue of discontentment. Why do you think we tend to diminish the significance of this sin?

- "Life's not fair." How should a Christian respond to this statement?

  If you are in a group, discuss possible ways one could us an unbeliever's sense that life is not fair to share the gospel. How can we show an unbeliever that their discontentment is actually a blessing? What does it ultimately point to?

- In this lesson, what does the Belgic Confession teach us about God's goodness and sovereignty?

  If you are in a group, have the members discuss Mrs. Kruger's illustration of the dot on the board and how that has affected their understanding of God's sovereignty.

PRAYER

Commit what you have learned from God's Word in this lesson to prayer.

- Praise God for accomplishing salvation for His people in Christ.
- Confess that you have grumbled and complained against a good and loving God.
- Thank God for showing mercy to you instead of judging you in accordance with your sin.
- Ask God to mortify the sin of covetousness in your heart.

REVIEW QUIZ

Use these multiple-choice questions to measure what you learned from this lesson.

1. What does Mrs. Kruger say is the source of our discontentment and covetousness?
   a. Unbelief
   b. Laziness
   c. Apathy
   d. Pride

2. Which of the following was *not* given as a source of discontentment?
   a. Unbelief in the character of God
   b. Unbelief in our true home
   c. Unbelief in our wisdom
   d. Unbelief in our true purpose

3. What two characteristics of God are we primarily distrusting when we are discontent?
   a. His sovereignty and His judgement
   b. His goodness and His love
   c. His justice and His judgment
   d. His sovereignty and His goodness

4. What does Mrs. Kruger say that covetousness is in regard to the heart?
   a. A heart divided between the world and eternity
   b. A heart divided between two gods
   c. A heart divided between good and evil
   d. A heart divided between two religions

5. Discontentment comes from disbelief in who God is.
   a. True
   b. False

6. What image does Mrs. Kruger use to illustrate how small our knowledge is compared to God's knowledge?
   a. A grain of sand on the beach
   b. A person in a crowd
   c. A drop in a bucket
   d. A dot on a wall

Answer Key—What Causes Discontentment?

Before the Video

What Do You Think?

These are personal questions. The answers should be based on your own knowledge and experience.

Scripture Reading

- How does our estimation of our own wisdom affect our contentment?

  When we view ourselves as possessing more wisdom than God, it leads us to distrust Him and His plans for us. We can never be content with this improper view of God and ourselves. This passage teaches us to not be wise in our own eyes but instead to fear the Lord, trusting that our contentment only comes from Him.

During the Video

Discontentment

- How is discontentment a reflection of unbelief?

  A heart that believes God and is under the authority of His Word will demonstrate that belief with outward contentment. It is similar to what Jesus says in Luke 6:45 that out of the abundance of the heart the mouth speaks. If we do not believe God and hold fast to His promises, then we will see the effects of unbelief in a life of discontentment.

- How should the understanding that this world is not our home inform how we live in the present?

  As it relates to our contentment, we should enjoy this world for what it is and be content with where the Lord has us and how He is using us. We can be more content in this world because we expect less out of it. Our true rest, hope, and longing should be for Christ and to be with Him in our true home. This means we can be joyful in this life because we are not putting all of hope in this world. We still have an obligation to be good and faithful stewards of this world, but we must remember that our true home is a future home.

Purpose in Christ

- How is it good news that Christ's purpose for us is not to have our best life now?

  God is sanctifying us and making us more into the image of Christ as new creations in Christ. This necessarily means that this present time of sanctification *cannot give us the same joy and satisfaction that our glorification will. We should take comfort that God has a plan and is working all things together for the ultimate good of those who are in Christ. Our best life is still to come.*

- How can misunderstanding our purpose in the body of Christ produce discontentment?

  Our tendency can be to only value the purposes that Christ has prepared for others and view our purpose as insignificant. If we are always only looking at what Christ is doing in others, not only does discontentment grow within us, but so does covetousness. We are called to trust Christ and the purpose He has for us and to value ourselves in accordance with the calling to which we have been called, which is union with Christ in His body.

After the Video

- What does discontentment say about our view of the cross?

  Discontentment disregards what Christ has already done for us, particularly at the cross, and only looks to what else Christ can do for us. A discontent heart looks at the cross as an insufficient demonstration of God's love. But the love of God through the cross should calm our worries and anxieties in this life. Discontentment, then, is a heart issue that should be taken seriously by Christians.

- "Life's not fair." How should a Christian respond to this statement?

  A Christian has a greater understanding than anyone of just how unfair life is. We were deserving of nothing but condemnation and death but instead had all of our sin imputed to Christ and Christ's righteousness imputed to us. This truth causes Christians to live in gratitude and humility. We have been justified, adopted, and have received eternal life in Christ—all as a gift of God's grace. "Life's not fair" is good news for the Christian, because we are sinners saved by grace.

- In this lesson, what does the Belgic Confession teach us about God's goodness and sovereignty?

  The Belgic Confession teaches that God sovereignly rules and governs His people according to His holy will, so that nothing can happen to them without God's appointment. God's sovereignty over His creatures should bring consolation to the believer because we know that this God, who is perfectly sovereign, is also perfectly good. Therefore, we can rest content in our Lord because He is working all things together for our good and His glory. This truth is at the heart of true contentment.

REVIEW QUIZ

1. **A.**
   Mrs. Kruger emphasized that unbelief leads to discontentment. When we are discontent, we are not trusting in the wisdom and plan of God. Distrusting God is unbelief in God.

2. **C.**

   Mrs. Kruger mentioned three sins that cause our discontentment; unbelief in the character of God, unbelief in our true home, and unbelief in our true purpose. We should lean upon the Lord's wisdom and knowledge, having a proper view of our wisdom in comparison to His.

3. **D.**

   When we are discontent, we question God's sovereignty and His goodness. We are believing that God can't be in control of our lives because what is happening to us is not what we would have chosen. We also question His goodness by assuming that He can't be good because a trial has befallen us.

4. **B.**

   Mrs. Kruger said, "Covetousness is a heart divided between two gods." When we covet and desire something that we shouldn't, we make the object of our desire an idol. The heart is then divided between our false notions about God and the idolatry of covetousness.

5. **A.**

   This statement is true because the entirety of the hope of the Christian is dependent upon the character of God. If God is not who He says He is, then we have no reason to be content in this life. If God is not working in us now and preparing us for future glory, then covetousness is the most logical option. Thankfully, God is who He says He is, and we can trust Him and be content in this life.

6. **D.**

   The dot on the wall is a poignant image because it demonstrates the chasm between our knowledge and God's knowledge. God's knowledge and wisdom are infinite and incomprehensible, and it is this truth that should cause us to examine the way we think about ourselves, making us humbler.

6

Patterns of Discontentment

INTRODUCTION

The sin of discontentment follows a discernable pattern. We see this pattern throughout Scripture and in our own lives. In this session, Melissa Kruger explains through the stories of Eve and Achan how discontentment follows the pattern of seeing, coveting, taking, and hiding. She also explains how to break the pattern of discontentment before it starts.

LEARNING GOALS

When you have finished this lesson, you should be able to:

- Understand and name the steps in the pattern of discontentment
- List the three ways that coveting is alive that we often don't think of
- Narrate the stories of Eve and Achan

KEY IDEAS

- Scripture provides us with a pattern of discontentment that can help us guard against it in our own lives.
- The temptation of covetousness begins with our eyes, so it is the first place we must address to break the pattern of discontentment.

REFLECTION & DISCUSSION QUESTIONS

Before the Video

What Do You Think?

Take a moment to answer the following questions. They will prepare you for the lecture.

- How differently would your life look each day if you accepted with joy everything that happens as according to God's will?

- What particular things are you prone to covet? In what environments are you most susceptible to this sin?

Scripture Reading

Then Joshua said to Achan, "My son, give glory to the Lord God of Israel and give praise to him. And tell me now what you have done; do not hide it from me." And Achan answered Joshua, "Truly I have sinned against the Lord God of Israel, and this is what I did: when I saw among the spoil a beautiful cloak from Shinar, and 200 shekels of silver, and a bar of gold weighing 50 shekels, then I coveted them and took them. And see, they are hidden in the earth inside my tent, with the silver underneath."

—Joshua 7:19–21

- What can we learn from Achan about confessing sins when confronted?

During the Video

Answer the following questions while you watch the video. They will guide you through the lecture.

Stories of Discontent   *0:00–7:59*

- What was the essence of Satan's lie to Eve in the garden of Eden?

- What does the story of Achan tell us about the thought pattern of discontentment?

Discontentment and Comparison   *7:59–23:52*

- What is the Christian's responsibility when it comes to what they see and interact with?

- What is the danger of comparing our circumstances with someone who is in worse or better circumstances?

After the Video

Answer the following questions after you have finished the lecture. They will help you identify and summarize the major points.

- How does God often use the mundane moments in life to bring us to greater joy? How do we often use these moments to justify sinful behavior?

If you are in a group, discuss Mrs. Kruger's question from the lecture: "How different would your life be each day if you accepted with joy whatever the Lord brought?"

- What does Mrs. Kruger mean when she talks about our proclivity to take from others?

If you are in a group, discuss in what ways you can give to others in your life. Reflect on the following question. Is there anyone you are aware of who has a need that God can use you to provide?

- How does coveting affect worship?

If you are in a group, read 2 Kings 17:41. How does this passage teach you the importance of setting a godly example? How does it teach you the importance of the Christian home?

PRAYER

Commit what you have learned from God's Word in this lesson to prayer.

- Praise God that He is forgiving and long-suffering.
- Confess how you are prone to give into temptation because you do not trust God as we ought.
- Thank God for giving you loved ones to encourage you and help you resist temptation.
- Ask God to change the selfishness of your heart and cultivate righteous desires.

REVIEW QUIZ

Use these multiple-choice questions to measure what you learned from this lesson.

1. What is the pattern of discontentment?
    a. See, covet, hide, and praise
    b. Covet, ask, obtain, and praise
    c. See, covet, take, and hide
    d. Want, ask, get, and keep

2. What two characteristics of God does Satan attack when he tempts Eve?
    a. His faithfulness and His love
    b. His knowledge and His justice
    c. His goodness and His faithfulness
    d. His sovereignty and His goodness

3. What point in the pattern of discontentment should we pay extra attention to, so as to stop it before it starts?
    a. See
    b. Hide
    c. Covet
    d. Take

4. What is one thing that we cannot cut out of our lives, even if we are tempted toward coveting?
    a. Leisure time
    b. Recreation activities
    c. Our church community
    d. Family gatherings

5. When we are going through a hard time, we should always remind ourselves that someone out there has it worse than we do.
    a. True
    b. False

6. Which of the following is *not* an example presented by Mrs. Kruger of taking from others?
    a. Taking by failing to rejoice with someone
    b. Taking by giving too much of yourself
    c. Taking by failing to mourn with someone
    d. Taking by failing to spend time alone with the Lord

Answer Key—Patterns of Discontentment

REFLECTION & DISCUSSION QUESTIONS

Before the Video

What Do You Think?

These are personal questions. The answers should be based on your own knowledge and experience.

Scripture Reading

- What can we learn from Achan about confessing sins when confronted?

  The Lord wants us to turn from temptation and flee from sin. We do not always do this, however. Once we have been confronted with a sin or a place where we have coveted and fallen into the pattern of discontentment, it is important to confess and repent immediately and not continue to hide and flee from the consequences of our sin.

During the Video

Stories of Discontent

- What was the essence of Satan's lie to Eve in the garden of Eden?

  The essence of Satan's lie was to question both God's sovereignty and His goodness. By saying, "You will not surely die," he inserted doubt about whether God would do what He said He would do. In telling Eve that God knew that she would have her eyes opened and receive knowledge of good and evil, Satan insinuated that God was holding something back from her, making God out to be a liar.

- What does the story of Achan tell us about the thought pattern of discontentment?

  Achan's story is one that resonates with many of us. His people had lived for forty years without the possessions found in the cities. He perhaps thought that God had little need for this one robe, so he took it. This discontentment had catastrophic effects not only for himself but for his family and for several of the men who had gone into battle obedient to the Lord's command. Sin has far-reaching effects wherever it is present, and we should be always mindful of this.

Discontentment and Comparison

- What is the Christian's responsibility when it comes to what they see and interact with?

As Mrs. Kruger stated in this lesson, "Not all seeing is sin." We are not called to remove ourselves from the world and no longer take in and interact with the world around us in order to avoid sinning. Instead, we are called to be discerning and know where our weaknesses and insecurities are and to avoid sinful temptation wherever we can.

- What is the danger of comparing our circumstances with someone who is in worse or better circumstances?

The danger of comparing ourselves to others who may be less fortunate than us is that the source of our contentment can then become rooted in another's misfortunes. The same is true when we compare ourselves to others who are in better circumstances. We are to recognize that we do not know what other people are going through, even though things may look perfect on the outside. We should constantly be bringing our minds back to the fact that God is working in each of us in different ways and that we should pray for our neighbors instead of comparing ourselves to them.

After the Video

- How does God often use the mundane moments in life to bring us to greater joy? How do we often use these moments to justify sinful behavior?

It is in the mundane moments of everyday life that God helps us live out the theology that we learn. Through this process of mundane sanctification, the Lord produces greater patience and kindness and love, which in turn produce greater joy in Christ. On the other hand, it is our tendency to look at the little frustrations of life as an opportunity to justify being rude and impatient and unloving toward others. This is not the heart of a Christian, and we must always pray and fight against this inclination.

- What does Mrs. Kruger mean when she talks about our proclivity to take from others?

Taking from others usually takes the form of withholding from someone something that is due to them, such as failing to rejoice with others, failing to mourn with those who mourn, and failing to give generously to the church. When we take from others, what we are really doing is taking out our frustrations with God on other people. This reveals our own laziness and selfishness in that we refuse to do for others until we ourselves have been taken care of.

- How does coveting affect worship?

While we are born into this world as sinners, we also learn sin through the examples of those who are close to us. The idols of our parents can become the idols of our hearts, and we in turn can pass down these idols to our children. Mrs. Kruger shows the relationship that this vicious cycle of sin has to wrong worship in 2 Kings 17:41, where the children and grandchildren worshiped idols just as their parents and grandparents did. The Lord commands His people to have no other gods before Him, so when we make space for idols in our lives, it hinders our worship.

REVIEW QUIZ

1. **C.**

   The pattern of discontentment that Mrs. Kruger describes in this lesson is see, covet, take, and hide. We see something we want. We covet and make it an idol. We disobey, take it for our own, and then try to cover our sin by hiding it or ourselves from God.

2. **D.**

   The two characteristics of God that Satan attacks when he tempts are God's sovereignty and His goodness. Satan tempted Eve to question if God would really do what He said He WOULD do and to question if God actually intended for her own good.

3. **A.**

   In the pattern of discontentment, we should pay extra attention to the first step toward discontentment: see. As we go about our lives, we must be cautious of what we are seeing and how we are seeing it. If we see something and have covetous desires, we need remove ourselves from that thing. Our desire should be to stop the pattern before it starts.

4. **C.**

   While it is important to stop the pattern of discontent at seeing, it is important to note that we cannot cut out our church community just because we are seeing something that cause our covetous desires to arise. It is through the church that the Lord ministers to us and helps us to put our covetousness to death.

5. **B.**

   Sometimes we can gain perspective by reassuring ourselves that someone else has harder trials than we do. However, we are to be joyful in spite of our circumstances, not just because someone has it worse than we do.

6. **B.**

   Taking by giving too much of yourself is not a way presented that we can take from others. Mrs. Kruger says that we can take from others joy by not rejoicing with them, we can take from others mourning by not mourning with them, we can take from the church community by failing to give generously, we can take from others by failing to spend time with the Lord to gain wisdom to help them, and finally, we can take by gossiping and always talking about ourselves.

7

An Example of Contentment

INTRODUCTION

As we strive to find biblical contentment, there are many examples to look to in Scripture, but Jesus is the only perfect example. Jesus is our one unblemished example of contentment. In this lesson, the temptation of Jesus in the wilderness is highlighted to give believers hope for how to overcome temptations and discontentment. It was His perfect contentment that led to His perfect obedience.

LEARNING GOALS

When you have finished this lesson, you should be able to:

- List three aspects of Jesus' temptation
- Understand the role of Scripture in the fight against temptation
- Describe the three ways that Satan tempted Jesus

KEY IDEAS

- Jesus is the perfect example of contentment, and because of this, He breaks the sin pattern of our discontentment.
- Jesus' perfect contentment was what led to His perfect obedience.
- Obedience does not come from perfect circumstances; we obey despite circumstances.
- In order to be obedient people, we must be in God's Word.

REFLECTION & DISCUSSION QUESTIONS

Before the Video

What Do You Think?

Take a moment to answer the following questions. They will prepare you for the lecture.

- Was there a time in your life that discontentment led to disobedience to God? What happened because of this disobedience?

- Do you respond to temptation like Eve or like Jesus? Think of an example of each in your life.

Scripture Reading

We must not put Christ to the test, as some did and were destroyed by serpents, nor grumble, as some of them did and were destroyed by the Destroyer. Now these things happened to them as an example, but they were written down for our instruction, on whom the end of the ages has come. Therefore let anyone who thinks he stands take heed lest he fall. No temptation has overtaken you that is not common to man. God is faithful, and he will not let you be tempted beyond your ability, but with the temptation he will also provide the way of escape, that you may be able to endure it.

—1 Corinthians 10:9–13

- How does this passage show God's mercy to us?

During the Video

Answer the following questions while you watch the video. They will guide you through the lecture.

Circumstances of Temptation   *0:00–11:23*

- What do the circumstances of Eve's temptation and Christ's temptation tell us about our strength and Christ's strength?

- How does understanding the methods that Satan uses to tempt help us withstand when we are being tempted?

Jesus' Example of Contentment   *11:23–22:30*

- Why is it that being people of God's Word is so vital in our fight against temptation?

- How is Christ's active obedience good news in our fight against temptation?

After the Video

Answer the following questions after you have finished the lecture. They will help you identify and summarize the major points.

- How does our adoption as Christians affect our contentment?

  If you are in a group, discuss why you think it is that we live like orphans instead of children of the living God.

- In what ways does Christ's power affect our prayers?

  If you are in a group, discuss how your prayers can exude more dependence upon Christ to bring about His purposes.

- How does 2 Peter 1:3 encourage us to press forward towards obedience?

  If you are in a group, have the members name some other passages of Scripture that comfort them and encourage them to carry on in their Christian walk.

PRAYER

Commit what you have learned from God's Word in this lesson to prayer.

- Praise God for giving us Jesus as the perfect example of contentment.
- Confess ways in which you do not trust that Christ's righteousness is sufficient for you.
- Thank God for being merciful to you and providing escape in the midst of temptation.
- Ask God to help you to read, study, memorize, and believe Scripture.

REVIEW QUIZ

Use these multiple-choice questions to measure what you learned from this lesson.

1. What does Mrs. Kruger say Christ demonstrates concerning obedience in the midst of hard times?
   a. Obedience is possible during hard times.
   b. Obedience is necessary during hard times.
   c. Obedience is impossible during hard times.
   d. Obedience is not required during hard times.

2. Out of what kind of well is obedience going to spring?
   a. A well of love
   b. A well of peace
   c. A well of belief
   d. A well of knowledge

3. Which of the following is *not* an aspect of Jesus' temptation?
   a. The circumstances of His temptation
   b. The nature of His temptation
   c. The method He used to fight temptation
   d. The people that were with him during His temptation

4. Which of the following is *not* a way that Jesus was tempted?
   a. To prove He was the Son of God by turning stones to bread
   b. To throw Himself off the temple and have angels protect Him
   c. To bow down and worship Satan for the kingdoms of the world
   d. To heal His own wounds in demonstration of His power

5. God gives us every resource we need to trust in Him and resist temptation.
   a. True
   b. False

6. What analogy does Mrs. Kruger use to show that temporary things cannot give us eternal satisfaction?
   a. A child drinking from an empty cup
   b. A dog digging a hole to nowhere
   c. A man trying to eat the wind
   d. A plant with no roots

Answer Key— An Example of Contentment

REFLECTION & DISCUSSION QUESTIONS

Before the Video

What Do You Think?

These are personal questions. The answers should be based on your own knowledge and experience.

Scripture Reading

- How does this passage show God's mercy to us?

  God's mercy is shown to us during temptations in that He will never tempt us past what we can endure, and He always provides a way of escape. We can remain steadfast in the midst of temptation because we know that our God cares for us and will come to our aid when we call upon Him. Additionally, He has given us His Word for our instruction.

During the Video

Circumstances of Temptation

- What do the circumstances of Eve's temptation and Christ's temptation tell us about our strength and Christ's strength?

  Eve's circumstances were very ideal. She had all the food she could ever want, she lived in a perfect and cultivated garden, and she had great companionship with her husband. Yet, with every reason and incentive to live in obedience, she sinned. Jesus' circumstances were not ideal, yet He obeyed. This shows us that independent of circumstances we are weak and needy sinners. It also shows that independent of circumstances, Jesus is our perfect and faithful Mediator.

- How does understanding the methods that Satan uses to tempt help us withstand when we are being tempted?

  It should be a comfort to know that Satan is not innovative in his methods of temptation. The way that he tempted Eve is the same way that he tempted Jesus, and it's the same way that he tempts us. Understanding this, we can look to Jesus as our perfect example of obedience in the face of temptation. We are to saturate ourselves in the Word and in prayer and look to Christ working through His Spirit to strengthen us and help us in the time of temptation.

Jesus' Example of Contentment

- Why is it that being people of God's Word is so vital in our fight against temptation?

One of the means that the enemy will use to lead us to temptation is Scripture itself. It is only people who firmly believe all of God's Word, study it, meditate upon it, memorize it, and pray it who will be able to withstand temptation and be able to discern truth from half-truth. We must be people who not only know Scripture but love Scripture. If we do not live by the Word, then we will perish by the allure of our desires. This is the example that Christ set for His people.

- How is Christ's active obedience good news in our fight against temptation?

   When we think of Christ's work of accomplishing salvation, our minds often go directly to the cross, and there is good reason for that. But we must remember that the reason that the cross was effective was because Christ lived a life of perfect righteousness. Christ could be the perfect sacrifice because He led the perfect life. It was Christ's perfect obedience that was given to us, and that is good news for the Christian. We are able to fight against temptation and sin because our Lord has already won the fight. We have been freed from the dominion of sin and can now live in light of the good news.

After the Video

- How does our adoption as Christians affect our contentment?

   Our condition as sinners is so dire that we are incapable of realizing how much God loves us apart from His power. God's act of adopting and bringing His people into His family demonstrates the vastness of His goodness and love. It makes sense that we would find this truth hard to believe, but it is precisely because this is true that we can rest assured in the promises of God. Contentment flows from assurance in God and His promises, and so our adoption is one of the greatest acts of God's faithfulness that we can look back on and remember in times of trial and temptation.

- In what ways does Christ's power affect our prayers?

   When Paul said, "I can do all things through him who strengthens me" (Phil. 4:13), he was speaking of Christ's power to aid us in our contentment. If we are content in Christ's power to bring about change, then we will rightly turn away from ourselves and cast our worries upon Him in prayer. Our prayer should be that He would work powerfully in us to walk in a manner worthy of the Lord in faithfulness.

- How does 2 Peter 1:3 encourage us to press forward toward obedience?

   Second Peter 1:3 reveals that God has given us "all things that pertain to life and godliness." Therefore, everything that we will ever need to live obediently in contentment is fully ours already as a gift of God's grace. This should make us a people who abound in hope and confidence because we know that we are more than conquerors in Christ. Christ is more than just our example in righteousness, He is our righteousness.

REVIEW QUIZ

1. **A.**

   Obedience is possible in the midst of even the hardest times. Jesus was the perfect example of this. Never has anyone endured a more difficult experience than Jesus. The full weight of God's wrath was upon Him, and He was obedient through it all.

2. **C.**

   Obedience is going to spring from a well of belief. We cannot obey God if we do not believe in Him. First, we believe; then we obey. You cannot have one without the other.

3. **D.**

   The circumstances of Christ's temptation, the nature of His temptation, and the method that He used to resist the temptations were all discussed, but not the people who were with Him during His temptation.

4. **D.**

   Jesus was not tempted to heal His own wounds. Jesus was tempted three times: to turn stones into bread, to have the angels save Him, and to bow down and worship Satan in exchange of the kingdoms of the world. The temptation of Christ is detailed in Matthew 4, Mark 1, and Luke 4.

5. **A.**

   God has given us every resource we need to trust in Him and to resist and flee from temptation in His Word. Moreover, He promises that we will never be tempted beyond what we can bear.

6. **C.**

   Mrs. Kruger uses the analogy of a man opening his mouth and trying to eat the wind to satisfy his hunger. He is still hungry because the wind cannot satisfy his hunger. This analogy is used to show that temporary things cannot satisfy our eternal hunger.

8

Cultivating Contentment

INTRODUCTION

Having a robust knowledge of contentment is beneficial only insofar as we know how to cultivate it in our lives. It is a good thing to learn about these truths, but these truths go hand in hand with learning how to cultivate contentment in our own lives. So how do we do this? In this lesson, Melissa Kruger concludes her series on contentment by giving practical ways to apply what has been taught to cultivate contentment.

LEARNING GOALS

When you have finished this lesson, you should be able to:

- State and describe the pattern of belief that leads to contentment
- Describe ways in which we can cultivate contentment in our lives
- List three ways that Scripture describes the Christian life

KEY IDEAS

- Not only is there a pattern of discontentment, but there is also a pattern of contentment: seek, desire rightly, give generously, and confess freely.
- We must be in the Word and in the church in order to faithfully live out the pattern of contentment.
- If you are struggling with contentment in the moment, look back at what Christ did on the cross, and then look forward to your eternal home with Him.

REFLECTION & DISCUSSION QUESTIONS

Before the Video

What Do You Think?

Take a moment to answer the following questions. They will prepare you for the lecture.

- What are things that you have found to be helpful in gaining contentment in your life?

- Are you a generous person? Or is giving freely difficult for you?

Scripture Reading

Pray then like this: "Our Father in heaven, hallowed be your name. Your Kingdom come, your will be done, on earth as it is in heaven. Give us this day our daily bread, and forgive us our debts, as we also have forgiven our debtors. And lead us not into temptation, but deliver us from evil."

—Matthew 6:9–13

- How is Lord's Prayer helpful to use as a model for all of our prayers?

During the Video

Answer the following questions while you watch the video. They will guide you through the lecture.

Cultivating Contentment   0:00–6:00

- What is the primary tool that Mrs. Kruger prescribes for our continual use in seeking the Lord?

- What role does the church play in the cultivation of contentment?

Cultivating New Desires   6:00–23:42

- What does Mrs. Kruger say is our greatest problem, as it relates to our desires?

- How does praying the Lord's Prayer reorient our desires?

After the Video

Answer the following questions after you have finished the lecture. They will help you identify and summarize the major points.

- Why does Mrs. Kruger say it can be terrifying to accept the Lord's will as best?

  If you are in a group, consider the five axioms of contentment quoted by Elizabeth Elliot: First, "Allow yourself to complain of nothing, not even the weather." Second, "Never picture yourself to yourself under any circumstance in which you are not." Third, "Never compare your lot with another." Fourth, "Never allow yourself to dwell on the wish that this or that had been or were otherwise than it is. God almighty loves you better and more wisely than you love yourself." Fifth, "Never dwell on tomorrow. Remember it is God's, not yours. The heaviest part of sorrow is often to look forward to it. The Lord will provide." Which of these do you have the most trouble practicing?

- How does giving generously relate to contentment?

  If you are in a group, read 2 Corinthians 9:6–15. Discuss the importance of giving and what it means to be a cheerful giver.

- What is the fundamental difference between confessing our sins and hiding from them?

  If you are in a group, have the members discuss what makes it the hardest for them to confess their sins and repent when they have acted wrongly.

PRAYER

Commit what you have learned from God's Word in this lesson to prayer.

- Praise God for His good and perfect will in all circumstances throughout all generations.
- Confess that your natural inclination is to hide from your sins instead of confessing them.
- Thank God for the means of grace that He provides to help you in your struggle against sin.
- Ask God to make your heart more willing to repent instead of running away from your sin.

REVIEW QUIZ

Use these multiple-choice questions to measure what you learned from this lesson.

1. What does Mrs. Kruger say to do every day in regard to your prayer life?
   a. Pray for yourself last
   b. Pray the Lord's Prayer
   c. Pray only when you remember
   d. Pray for only short periods of time

2. What is the pattern of belief that leads to contentment?
   a. Seek, confess freely, and praise God
   b. Praise God, desire rightly, give generously, and confess freely
   c. Seek, desire rightly, give generously, and confess freely
   d. Give generously, desire rightly, seek, and praise God

3. Where does the battle for contentment begin?
   a. In the mind
   b. In the heart
   c. In the Bible
   d. In the world

4. What does Mrs. Kruger say is the greatest problem in regard to our desire?
   a. We desire bad things for others.
   b. We desire wrong things.
   c. We desire far too much.
   d. We desire far too little.

5. We should have no desire to live for ourselves, but we should desire to live completely and perfectly for God.
   a. True
   b. False

6. Which of the following is *not* a way that Scripture describes the Christian life?
   a. Childbirth
   b. A battle
   c. A race
   d. A construction project

Answer Key—Cultivating Contentment

REFLECTION & DISCUSSION QUESTIONS

Before the Video

What Do You Think?

> *These are personal questions. The answers should be based on your own knowledge and experience.*

Scripture Reading

- How is Lord's Prayer helpful to use as a model for all of our prayers?

    The Lord's Prayer is helpful in directing the focus of all of our prayers. We acknowledge and praise God for who He is, and the desires of our heart flow from that foundation. The Lord directs us to Himself so that we may know to come to Him for all that we need.

During the Video

Cultivating Contentment

- What is the primary tool that Mrs. Kruger prescribes for our continual use in seeking the Lord?

    The primary tool that we have for combating spiritual lethargy and growing in maturity in Christ is the Word of God. Being people who are devoted to and saturated in the Word of God is the only way to know God better and seek the true God as opposed to a god of our own making. Spending time in the Word needs to be a priority if any growth is to be expected.

- What role does the church play in the cultivation of contentment?

    The church is a means of giving the Word of God to the people of God. We also need to see the Word lived out in a community of people, and the church is the primary place that we can take part in this. We are not left to ourselves to grow as Christians, but we are brought into a body of believers who are used to teach us, challenge us, love us, study with us, and pray with us as we contribute to the needs of one another.

Cultivating New Desires

- What does Mrs. Kruger say is our greatest problem, as it relates to our desires?

    Our greatest problem is that we desire far too little rather than too much. We need to be a people who desire to know Jesus more than anything else. All things have their being in Christ, He owns it all, and yet our desires are so often for the gift rather than the Giver. Our prayers should reflect a proper desire, praying that the Lord would renew and properly order our desires each day.

- How does praying the Lord's Prayer reorient our desires?

  The prelude of this prayer reminds us, first, that God is God and no one else. He is the One who is transcendent and dwells in heaven. The prelude also says that our God is imminent in that He condescends to us so that we can approach Him as our heavenly Father. When we know that God is both God and Father, we can trust Him, able to pray that His will be done on earth as it is in heaven. Our desires are being transformed as Christians to the degree that we desire His will to be done and His kingdom to come as opposed to our own.

After the Video

- Why does Mrs. Kruger say it can be terrifying to accept the Lord's will as best?

  It can be terrifying to accept the Lord's will as best if we think that we know ourselves better than God knows us. It is a terrifying reality to accept if we believe that we can do all things well before God. It is the Christian who is calmed and rests contently in the fact that the purposes of God are far greater than anything he could ever imagine for himself.

- How does giving generously relate to contentment?

  What we hold on to is what we care about most in life. For many of us, we think that accumulating and amassing more things will make us more satisfied and content, when actually the exact opposite is true. There is nothing wrong with wealth or possessions, but to hoard what we amass is to make a good thing an ultimate thing. Christians give generously of all that they are and all that they have because they know that they do not have anything that they did not first receive. To see possessions as a gift received from God allows us to treasure the Lord in our hearts and to give as we have been given to. This heart change will naturally lead to contentment with the possessions we have and not to valuing them above all else, which is idolatry.

- What is the fundamental difference between confessing our sins and hiding from them?

  Hiding from our sin is the attempt to rationalize our sin and explain them away, as if our sin isn't really sin. On the other hand, to confess our sin is to recognize our sin for what it is and to admit that we have acted wickedly and rebelled against our holy and good God. The ultimate difference, then, between confessing our sins and hiding from them is the difference between pride and humility.

REVIEW QUIZ

1. **B.**

   Mrs. Kruger says to pray the Lord's Prayer every day. The Lord's Prayer is a helpful tool in guiding our prayers and focusing our desires on God's will and His kingdom.

2. **C.**

   The new pattern of belief is seek, desire rightly, give generously, and confess freely. We must seek the Word and the church, desire righteous and good things, give of ourselves and our possessions generously, and finally, confess our discontentment to God and to others.

3. **A.**

   The battle for contentment begins in the mind. We should pay close attention to our thoughts and the things that we consider. This is where both contentment and discontentment begin.

4. **D.**

   In this lesson, Mrs. Kruger says that our greatest problem with our desires is that we desire far too little, not far too much. We do not desire enough of the good things that the Lord has prepared for us.

5. **A.**

   The life of the world is defined by self-centeredness, but the life of the Christian is defined by conformity to the image and will of our Creator and Lord.

6. **D.**

   "A construction project" is not a way in which Scripture refers to the Christian life. Scripture refers to the Christian life as a battle, a race, and childbirth in many different places.